# HOW TO SURVIVE UNIVERSITY

HOW TO SURVIVE UNIVERSITY

Research by Sophie Martin

Summersdale Publishers Ltd
46 West Street
Chichester
West Sussex
PO19 1RP
UK

www.summersdale.com

Printed and bound in Malta

ISBN: 978-1-84953-890-9

Substantial discounts on bulk quantities of Summersdale books are available to corporations, professional associations and other organisations. For details contact general enquiries: telephone: +44 (0) 1243 771107 or email: enquiries@summersdale.com.

# HOW TO SURVIVE UNIVERSITY

## an essential POCKET GUIDE

### Tamsin King

summersdale

# INTRODUCTION

You've been waiting for the time you head off to university since you started school and now that you've got the grades (well done!), and a place on your chosen course, you're so close to experiencing student life. Helping you to make the most of your time there, this little book is packed with information and advice, including household hacks and how to personalise your room, DIY ideas for all your fancy dress needs, all-round university tips – from budgeting to note-taking – and ways to beat exam stress.

It's time to wave goodbye to free home-cooked meals and say hello to freedom!

# SORT OUT YOUR STUFF

Going to university is symbolic of a new beginning. So why not start afresh with your wardrobe too and have a clear-out of all the clothes and shoes you've hoarded? After all, you won't need that signed school shirt any more!

Don't just throw away your unwanted clothes, though – think about who else might appreciate receiving them. Contact your friends and family, and organise a mini sale at your house (with the homeowner's permission, of course!) or give them away to charity. You could even try to sell online the items that look like new or, in some cases, still have their tags on. Facebook sale pages are often good if you want to get rid of your clutter quickly and without the hassle of postage and packaging, but expect to charge a cheaper price than you would if you were to sell on eBay.

# WONDER RATHER THAN DOUBT IS THE ROOT *of all* KNOWLEDGE.

★ *Abraham Joshua Heschel* ★

# ★ FANCY DRESS IDEAS ★

## TOGA PARTY

No prizes for guessing the costume you need for this one. Here are some simple steps you can follow to create a toga.

**1** Hold one of the corners of a plain bed sheet (preferably for a single bed so it doesn't swamp you!) with your left hand; leave around 15–20 cm between the tip of the corner and your grip so you have something to pin later. Bring it to your left shoulder.

**2** Drape the sheet across your chest and tuck it under your right arm so it is a snug fit against your chest.

**3** At this stage you will notice if the sheet is going to be too long (ideally, it should be knee-length) and if that is the case, fold it until it is the correct length and secure with safety pins.

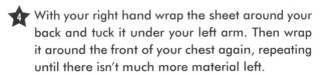

**4** With your right hand wrap the sheet around your back and tuck it under your left arm. Then wrap it around the front of your chest again, repeating until there isn't much more material left.

**5** Now bring the second corner up over your back so it meets with the first end. Secure them together with a brooch, pin or simple knot.

**6** Fix the layers tightly with safety pins. Do a wiggle and a jiggle to make sure that the toga won't fall off and isn't uncomfortable.

**7** Top off the look with a gold belt (or gold material), some sandals and a bunch of grapes.

**8** Provided you don't spill red wine down it, you could even wash it after so it's ready to go back on your bed.

wrap

pin

wiggle to
check it
doesn't slip

# HANGOVER CURES DEBUNKED

## *Spirits to Beer, Never Fear*

## MYTH

Although there is some truth in this, it's got nothing to do with what's different about the two drinks' ingredients. In fact, it's really down to the volume of the drink and how much you consume. For instance, if you start off drinking singles with mixer and follow with pints of beer, your intake slows down, as it's a heavier drink and more likely to make you feel bloated, meaning that you'll drink less of the latter.

# ALCOHOL,
TAKEN IN

*sufficient quantities,*

## MAY PRODUCE
## ALL THE EFFECTS OF
*drunkenness.*

★ *Oscar Wilde* ★

# REMEMBER TO ENROL

After all the freshers' fair fun, don't forget to enrol! As well as missing out on using the uni's facilities, you won't be able to claim student discounts if you don't, as you won't have your student card. Speaking of which, always ask the sales assistant if the shop accepts NUS cards, as a lot of places don't advertise it.

# RECIPE FOR AN ITALIAN NIGHT IN

## SPAGHETTI BOLOGNESE
### SERVES FOUR

For those who haven't cooked this classic dish before, let it be the first recipe you try at uni. It's easy and delicious, and there's not too much of a risk of setting your halls on fire.

## INGREDIENTS

- 2 tbsp olive oil
- 1 onion, peeled and chopped
- 2 cloves garlic, peeled and finely chopped
- 500 g minced beef
- 1 tin chopped tomatoes

100 g mushrooms, washed and sliced
1 carrot, peeled and grated
2 rashers of bacon, cut into small pieces
1 large glass of red wine (optional)
1 tbsp tomato purée
375 ml beef stock
Salt
Pepper
Parmesan cheese to serve

1. Heat the oil in a large saucepan, then add the onion and garlic, and fry gently for five minutes, being careful not to burn them.

2. Add the minced beef and continue frying for a further ten minutes. Then add the remaining ingredients.

3. After your sauce has reduced, which takes around 20 minutes, serve with the pasta of your choice – it doesn't have to be spaghetti – and a sprinkling of Parmesan on top.

## TOP TIP

If you have Bolognese left over, you can freeze it for next time. To defrost, place in the fridge during the day and then reheat it until piping hot. You can even freeze the excess pasta if you're feeling super-economical, but it has to be al dente and mixed in with the sauce when frozen otherwise it will go sticky and starchy when you reheat.

# BUYING YOUR NOTEBOOKS

Before you start attending your lectures, you need to buy a notebook for each of your modules – that's if you prefer writing to typing. Don't just buy one notebook for everything, as you'll end up spending most of your revision time flicking through the pages, trying to find something specific that you briefly remember your lecturer saying… but which lecturer was it?! When choosing your notebooks, go for something practical – heavy cover boards and size A4 won't be suitable if you have to commute to uni, while blank pages will make your notes look like the work of a caveman. If you buy the same journal for each of your modules, remove the confusion of knowing which is which by colour-coding them. Use a different coloured felt-tip and shade in the edges of the pages so it's clear at a glance that you are picking up the correct one.

# ★ HOUSEHOLD HACK ★

You've been preparing for this moment for months and it's now in sight, but before moving day you need to be practical about how you will transport all your worldly goods. This hack is also handy for when you move out of halls to a student house. Whatever heavy items you may be taking with you, load them into a suitcase with wheels and pull it to wherever it needs to go. The last thing you need is to load up a heavy box only to have the bottom fall out on you – heavy things hurt when they land on your toes.

# DRINKING GAME
# TREE HOUSE!

## No secret password required

DIFFICULTY: ★

No doubt during your time at uni you'll be involved in some sort of pub crawl, where you'll be consuming copious amounts of alcohol in every public house in sight. You can continue the drinking frolics in between each destination too, with this fun drinking game.

The rules are simple: if someone shouts 'Tree house!' everyone must get both feet off the ground, e.g. up onto a step, a bench, a wall or, if you're feeling adventurous, a tree*. The last person to do so must buy the next round or, if you're playing at home, down their drink.

For a sillier twist, why not change the trigger word or even make it a phrase such as 'I like turtles!' or 'Rubber baby buggy bumpers!'

*The author and publisher hold no responsibility for any type of embarrassment caused by playing this game. As the mature adult (you're over 18 years old now) you must take into account: a) your level of sobriety/ inebriety, b) your flexibility and c) both of these – if you can't see and you're as stiff as a board, we would implore you to find the safety of something 1 cm above ground level.

# JOIN SOCIETIES

Although you will probably spend your first year blindly drunk or recuperating from the night before, try introducing a bit of variety into your life and join a society that matches your interests. There you can meet new people who have something in common with you and aren't in your classes or halls. It also enables you to gain more skills and gives you the confidence to network, which will all help in securing that dream job.

★ *Do what* ★
# YOU LOVE,
★ *love what* ★
# YOU DO.

# RECIPE FOR WHEN YOU'RE MISSING MUM'S HOME-COOKING

## SHEPHERD'S PIE

### SERVES THREE TO FOUR

Although this popular recipe might not match your mum's shepherd's pie – it wouldn't be fair to give you any false hope – it's pretty darn good.

## INGREDIENTS

2 tbsp olive oil
1 onion, peeled and chopped
1 clove of garlic, peeled and finely chopped
500 g minced lamb
1 tin chopped tomatoes (optional)
1 tbsp tomato purée
1 tsp mixed herbs

Salt
Pepper
5 medium potatoes, peeled

1. Heat the oil in a largish saucepan, add the onion and garlic, and fry for three or four minutes.

2. Add the meat and cook for another ten minutes. Then add the other ingredients, except for the potatoes, and simmer for 15 minutes.

3. While this is simmering, boil the potatoes (test them with a knife – the knife should pass through the potato easily), drain and then mash them with a knob of butter and a bit of milk.

4. Put the meat in an ovenproof dish and cover with the potato, then put under the grill until the mash browns.

## TOP TIP

You can freeze a shepherd's pie whole or cut it into sections and freeze them individually, giving you more freezer space and the correct portion sizes for when you come to reheat your dish. Freeze by allowing it to cool and covering with tin foil. To defrost, move the pie to the fridge and leave throughout the day, then reheat in the microwave or the oven until piping hot.

# ★ HOUSEHOLD HACK ★

If you struggled to leave anything behind when packing for uni then this is a game-changing hack for you.

Save the ring pulls from cans of soft drinks and beer, and thread them onto the hook of a hanger, letting them rest where the hook meets the hanger itself. You have now created a loop to attach another hanger, thus doubling the capacity.

# CHALLENGES ARE WHAT MAKE LIFE *interesting;* OVERCOMING THEM IS WHAT MAKES LIFE *meaningful.*

★ Joshua J. Marine ★

# GET YOUR
≈ S**T TOGETHER ≈

The first day of the first year at university: an exciting time shared with lots of new people and involving lots of drink. Get drunk and be merry, but be safe. There's nothing worse than not remembering that particular night, with the only recollection being your friends' accounts and social media. To stop yourself getting wasted, take it slowly, drink water after every alcoholic drink and try not to mix drinks too much.

# HANGOVER CURES DEBUNKED

## *Coffee Will Make You Feel Dandy*

## MYTH

When you wake up bleary-eyed and reach for the kettle, think again before you have your dose of coffee, or anything with lots of caffeine in for that matter. If consumed in relatively large amounts, it makes you even more dehydrated and could end up making you feel worse. Instead, if you want something hot, try some herbal tea, which is known to relieve nausea, and is packed with antioxidants, vitamins and minerals.

# PERSONALISE YOUR ROOM

It's difficult to personalise your room knowing that you have to return it to its previous state once you move out. Although you don't want to be refilling the holes you have made in the walls, you can still add a touch of colour and fun without the need for any filler. Do this by buying decals – transferable art for your walls that can be applied and removed with ease and no marks – which you can find online. From animals and glow-in-the-dark astrology to travel and typography, you will be able to make your room yours and then, at the end of the year, take them down without hassle.

If you still think your living space doesn't say enough about you, then buy some Command™ hooks (sticky-back hooks that don't strip the paint off the walls) so that you can still put up that picture of you with your family or bessies from back home.

# KEEPING YOUR KITCHEN SHELVES SHIPSHAPE

So you've divvied out shelf and storage space in the kitchen, and that leaves you with, well... not a lot of space. However, there are ways to be more economical with your designated areas by following these tips.

★ When you do a shop, don't be lured into the three-for-two/buy-ten-get-one-free offers unless you know that you won't waste the extra stock. Often supermarkets do these deals for food items that are perishable and with a short expiry date, meaning that it isn't physically possible to eat all the food, especially as most of the time you'll be cooking/eating for one.

★ Make a shopping list before you start browsing, as having no prompts will only lead to impulse purchases. It's easy to forget what's in our cupboards and we tend to buy more of the same thing unless we are aware of it.

★ Every month or two go through your fridge, freezer and cupboards, and make sure that everything that's gone off is thrown away. While you are doing this, rotate your food items so that the stuff closest to going off is at the front.

★ You can also keep a record of what foods have been sitting in your cupboards for a while but have been untouched. Cereals are often the worst culprit. If there are a few crumbs at the bottom of the packet, throw it away, as you probably won't eat them. However, if you have packets or tins that are unopened and still in date, take them to a food bank so you aren't being wasteful.

★ In order to maximise your space, place similar loose items into containers. So, your veg in one container, your eggs in another, and so on.

*A place for*
# EVERYTHING
AND
# EVERYTHING
# IN ITS PLACE.

★ *Mrs Beeton* ★

# RECIPE FOR TASTY FOOD ON A SHOESTRING

## ULTIMATE BEANS ON TOAST

### SERVES TWO

A classic recipe with a twist that is oh-so-simple, cheap and tasty.

## INGREDIENTS

   4 slices of bread – fresh is best
   1 tbsp olive oil
   1 onion, diced
   ½ tsp ground cumin
   ½ tsp ground coriander
   85 g semi-dried tomatoes from a jar,
      chopped if large
   400 g can baked beans
   2 eggs

Butter, for spreading (optional)
Freshly chopped coriander or parsley, to serve

1. Bring water to the boil in a saucepan for the eggs and toast the bread. Heat the oil in a frying pan, add the onion and gently cook for a few minutes until it starts to brown. Mix the spices into the pan and stir briefly. Add the tomatoes and beans, and cook until warm through.

2. Turn down the heat under the saucepan so the water is just simmering, then crack in the eggs and gently poach them* until the whites are firm but the yolks are still runny. Layer the beans onto the toast (buttered or unbuttered, as you wish) and place the eggs on top.

3. Serve with a sprinkle of extra cumin and coriander or parsley.

*see overleaf

## TOP TIPS TO POACH THE PERFECT EGG

1. Ensure that the egg is fresh.

2. Add a dash of vinegar to the water once simmering but never use salt.

3. Crack the egg into a ramekin or cup before adding to the pan.

4. Create a soft whirlpool in the water with a spoon before adding the egg.

5. Slowly tip the egg into the water, and cook for three minutes above a simmer but not at boiling point.

6. Remove with a slotted spoon and drain on kitchen paper before serving.

# GET YOUR
## S**T TOGETHER

Once you've arrived at uni and you've waved bye to your family, don't be alarmed if you feel a slight pang of loneliness. This is probably the first time you've lived away from home. While you are experiencing these weird alien emotions, so will everyone else – they might just be hiding them well. Instead of going to your room for some quiet time and to wallow in your homesickness, make the effort to sit down in your communal area. Your peers will soon follow suit. Making a habit of being in your room all the time will give the impression that you don't want to join in and you'll start to miss out on the events.

# If it scares you, IT MIGHT BE A GOOD THING TO TRY.

★ *Seth Godin* ★

# HEALTHY RECIPE TO MAKE UP FOR THE PIZZA YOU HAD THE PREVIOUS NIGHT

## CHICKEN NOODLES

### SERVES TWO

A nutritious, wholesome and hearty dish. Noodles are a low-GI food (which means they will make you feel fuller for longer), while chicken is high in protein and low in fat.

## INGREDIENTS

1 tbsp olive oil
4 chicken breasts, diced
1 garlic clove, crushed or sliced
1 red pepper, thinly sliced
1 green pepper, thinly sliced
5 spring onions, sliced
100 g bean sprouts
2 x 150 g packs dry noodles
3 tbsp oyster sauce

1. Heat the oil in a large frying pan, and stir-fry the chicken until golden and cooked all the way through.

2. Mix in the garlic and peppers, and cook for two minutes. Then add the spring onions, bean sprouts, noodles, sauce and five tablespoons of water, and stir-fry everything for another two minutes. Serve immediately.

# KEEP FIT

It's said that the average student adopts an unhealthier lifestyle during their time at university. A bad diet and little or no exercise often lead to a weaker immune system and feelings of lethargy, as well as weight gain. Here are a few tips on how to keep yourself fit and healthy.

★ Join university sports clubs – a great way to be active in an environment that is fun and social. Often there are tournaments you can partake in, if you are the competitive type, which allow you to travel to different universities and battle it out.

★ Join the uni gym – it costs less than a public gym and if you are unsure as to how much you'll use it, you can choose from different tiers.

★ Do exercise that you actually enjoy – there's no point going running if you find it dull and boring. Do something you like and you'll be more motivated.

★ Ask your friends if they want to exercise with you – if you don't want the commitment of being in a club, see if other people want to join you. Often you'll find that this helps you to: a) do it and b) push yourself.

★ Make a fitness timetable – decide on which days you will exercise and write them down, and remember that you don't have to do the same thing over and over. For example, a shorter run on Monday, yoga on Tuesday, a longer run on Wednesday, rest on Thursday, a swim on Friday, a long, brisk walk on Saturday and rest on Sunday.

★ As well as doing exercise, remember: you need to have a balanced diet too. Have your kebabs to abate a particularly nasty hangover, but counter this by eating healthily the rest of the time. It's best to cook your own meals so you know exactly what's going in them.

# THE SECRET OF
## *getting ahead*
# IS GETTING STARTED.

★ *Mark Twain* ★

# ★ HOUSEHOLD HACK ★

Pizza is good. But it's not so good when you come to reheat it in the microwave the next day. The dough goes from crisp to chewy and you end up gnashing and tearing away at the crust like a lion gnawing at a gazelle's hindquarters. But worry not: there is a way to stop this unsightly way of eating. When reheating your pizza in the microwave, also place a small glass containing some water in there and the crust will not dry out. If you still want to tear away at it like a lion, that's up to you.

# ★ FANCY DRESS IDEAS ★

## SCHOOL DISCO

There's guaranteed to be a geeky school disco at some point in your university life – probably within the first week, actually! Here are some tips on how to look the part without spending too much.

 School shirt or polo top – many of us will still fit into our old school uniform (you will get bonus points for authenticity) but if you don't have one at hand, you can always buy a pack of them without it costing too much, especially if you go splits with other people who need one.

 Black or grey trousers, shorts or skirt – you are bound to have some trousers lying around at home, so make sure that you take them with you. If you want to step it up a gear, then grey shorts with ankle-length white socks will attract a few looks.

**3** Marker pen – this will come in handy for drawing on freckles. If you have a polo shirt, you can also use the pen to get other people to write things on it. It's fun to take the pen out with you and see how many randomers you can persuade to write on you/your shirt (often ends up being the former). The next morning you are bound to find some obscure messages!

**4** Thick-rimmed glasses – if you don't have any of these, use a pair of 3D glasses and remove the plastic bits.

**5** The school tie – no ifs or buts, everyone should have one of these! But if you don't and neither do friends or family (ask those who are younger than you), then you can pick one up from a fancy dress shop for a couple of quid.

# HANGOVER CURES DEBUNKED

## H₂O, Alcohol, H₂O, Alcohol

**TRUE**

When you know it's student night, the main thing on your mind is alcohol. But if you think it's going to be a heavy one, drinking water in between your 'real' drinks will help to reduce (but not cure) your hangover symptoms. You may not get as slaughtered as you usually do but you'll certainly feel better for it in the morning.

## DRINKING GAME

# SPOONS

### *Does not involve any intimate cuddling*

DIFFICULTY: ★ ★

Players sit in a circle with the spoons in the centre, handles facing outwards and spoon ends touching. A deck of playing cards is then shuffled and four are dealt to each player. The aim of the game is to collect four of a kind (values, not suits!).

Everyone looks at their cards, selects a card to discard and places it face down to their left, picking up the discarded card from the player on their right. This continues throughout.

Once a player has four of a kind they can take a spoon from the centre and then resume playing as before, but always discarding the card they have just picked up so that they keep their set of four.

The person who doesn't manage to grab a spoon loses and must down their drink and sit out the next round.

Play starts again with one less set of cards and one less spoon and continues until only one spoon remains – the player who ends up with this is the winner.

# RECIPE FOR THAT HORRIBLE HANGOVER

## SUPER-DETOX SMOOTHIE

### SERVES TWO

Yes, it might be green and, yes, it might not look dissimilar to what has already come up this morning, but this smoothie will help you to recover from the deadliest of hangovers.

## INGREDIENTS

1 cup mixed berries, frozen
½ cup pineapple, papaya or mango, diced
1 cup dandelion greens
½ cup spinach
½ cup coconut milk
1–1½ cups coconut water

1. Place all the ingredients into a blender.

2. Blend until mixed thoroughly.

3. Pour into a glass and drink slowly, so you savour the taste and your body can absorb the nutrients.

# GET YOUR
## S**T TOGETHER

≈                              ≈

Don't fritter away all your student loan in the first week. There are other ways to make friends than buying everyone's drinks. It may be the first time that there are enough digits in your bank account to be able to buy a car but remember: this money has to last you until the next loan payment, which is usually further away than you think. You don't want to act like a stinge but at the same time don't be so frivolous that you have to contact the bank of Mum and Dad in your first week of being at uni.

# A PENNY *saved*

★ ★ ★ ★ IS A ★ ★ ★ ★

# PENNY EARNED.

★ *Benjamin Franklin* ★

# SMART BUDGETING

If this is your first time living away from home then it's probably the first time you've ever had to think about budgeting. The key is to consider it from the start, as it's very easy to hide from your finances and not even know how much you have in the bank. Firstly, set up an online banking account, if you haven't got one already. This allows you to look at all your transactions at the click of a button.

Secondly, create a spreadsheet with two columns. In the first one, write down your total income, such as your maintenance loan and grant, and your monthly salary if applicable. In the same column, write down your monthly outgoings, such as rent, bills, food and drink, travel and transport, clothes and shoes, going out, toiletries, laundry, holidays, presents, etc. In the second column write down how much you spend on each category, then add it up and work out if you are in minus figures. If that's the case, recalculate your average outgoings so that you aren't in the red and stick to them to avoid ending up overspending. When deciding where you can cut back, think about the outgoings that are essential and those that are less of a priority. Also consider where you are being wasteful with your money, for example overspending on the food shop or making too many impulse purchases.

# RECIPE FOR WHEN YOU WANT TO WALLOW IN CARB HEAVEN

## POTATO AND LEEK GRATIN

### SERVES SIX

This recipe is meant to serve six but that depends on the kind of day you've had...

## INGREDIENTS

600 ml chicken or vegetable stock
1 kg potatoes, thinly sliced
6 leeks, thinly sliced into rounds
25 g butter
3 tbsp double cream
Mature Cheddar cheese, grated

1.  Heat the oven to 200°C.

2.  Put the stock in a large pan and bring to the boil. Add the potatoes and the leeks, and bring back to the boil for five minutes. Drain well, reserving the stock in a jug. Meanwhile, butter a large baking dish.

3.  Layer up the potatoes and leeks – this doesn't have to be neat – seasoning as you go. Pour over 200 ml of the reserved stock, then spoon over the cream and cover with foil.

4.  Bake for 20 minutes, sprinkle the cheese on top and return to the oven without the foil, so the cheese browns, for another 20 minutes.

## **TOP TIP**

This is a really flexible recipe and you can throw all sorts of new ingredients in to change the flavour and bulk it up a bit. Although it's already a robust plateful, more is more when it comes to hungry student stomachs! For a smoky flavour, try chunks of bacon or mackerel. If you'd like to keep it vegetarian, try rubbing the dish with garlic and/or adding asparagus to the mix.

# ★ HOUSEHOLD HACK ★

If you like potatoes and you're a student, you will face some problems in the kitchen when you realise that, if you don't buy them loose, the pre-packed bags are too big for one person, even for someone who really loves the stuff. You can make your potatoes last longer with this hack.

To increase the shelf life of potatoes, just put an apple in the bag or container where you store them. The apple will not only provide some fruity company, but will also give off a gas that prevents the potatoes from sprouting.

Potatoes that look a little sorry for themselves are OK but when they've become shrivelled and wrinkly like a giant tortoise's knee joint then they are well and truly past it.

# KEEP YOUR ELECTRONIC FILES ORGANISED

Any assignment you are given will be done on your laptop or a PC. Make sure from the start that you have a system that will help you navigate your files with ease so that your study time isn't taken up by delving into your cyber black hole. Here are some tips on how to do this.

★ Delete unnecessary shortcuts and files that appear on the start screen. Booting up your computer with a fresh and motivated outlook only to find a deluge of files with no direct bearing to each other can make you feel defeated before you've even started.

★ Create a new folder called 'Uni work' or something similar before term begins. Within this folder you can add new sub-folders for the number of years you'll be studying and within these you can start to create sub-sub-folders once you know what modules you will be attending.

★ Make sure that your file names are relevant to the information that's in them. Be specific, too. For example, don't name them all after the module and leave it at that. Instead, insert the module name (acronyms often come in handy here), the lecture/seminar title and a date. This all helps when it comes to revising.

★ It's very likely that your lecturers will upload presentations, lecture notes and anything to do with the lecture you have attended onto the student portal. Unless you have a good memory, a lot of the time these resources are overlooked. If you are forgetful like me, it might be beneficial to download what you consider the most useful files onto your computer and store them in the relevant folder immediately after the lecture.

Tidy computer files are almost as satisfying as a tidy room!

# DON'T STAY PUT ON YOUR CAMPUS

In your first year there is so much time for you to discover your surroundings. As well as exploring the city you live in, take the chance to go further afield to the next city. Book your train tickets in advance and you'll make a bigger saving than if you bought them on the day. Before your visit, look up free things you can do and check money-saving sites, such as Groupon, for big discounts. If you plan to go in January and February, you will find a bigger variety of offers aimed at enticing people during the post-Christmas lull.

# THE GRASS
## IS GREENER
### *where you*
## WATER IT.

# PERSONALISE YOUR ROOM

Bring some of the outdoors inside with your own plants. Now that you have left home, you can become even more adult-like by adding some greenery to your room. Plants are very cheap and very easy to keep alive, provided you water them! Create your own plant pots by reusing empty tea caddies and filling them with soil. If you enjoy cooking, it might be worth growing herbs so you can use them in your food.

# PAPER-MANIA

Although paper handouts seem to be redundant, as most things are uploaded on university portals, they are great for scribbling extra details in the margins and are worth keeping for revision. I remember procuring at least five sheets per lecture/seminar and at first I was all in a mess about what to do with them. And I wasn't alone; my friends had the same issues with paper littering their furniture and floors, half of it ripped or covered in shoeprints, so that you could no longer read the material anyway.

In order to organise your paperwork neatly and systematically (so it actually means something to you when it comes to revising), try following these tips.

★ Set up a filing cabinet, drawer or concertina file and clearly mark the dividers with your module titles. (Avoid stacking your paper handouts in boxes, as it is more time-consuming to find what you are looking for.) A concertina file is often more accessible and easier to store away.

★ When you file your material, make sure that the documents are facing the same way, so you can see the course name clearly.

★ Ensure that you file your handouts as soon as you get back from your lectures, otherwise they may get lost at the bottom of your bag, never to be seen again! Additionally, before you file them it's handy to read the information as well as the notes you made in your notepad to let everything you learnt that day sink in.

WORK HARD, *be passionate* AND YOU WILL SUCCEED.

# RECIPE FOR SOME POSH NOSH IF YOU'RE COOKING FOR A DATE OR SPECIAL FRIEND

## CHICKEN WRAPPED IN PARMA HAM
### SERVES TWO

If love might possibly be in the air, it certainly will be after you've served this dish. And if that's not enough, try some of your hopelessly romantic lines. If that also fails, it's safe to say you are romantically hopeless.

## INGREDIENTS

2 boneless chicken breasts
6 slices prosciutto

2 tbsp olive oil
2 cloves garlic, crushed
Salt
Pepper
Green beans to serve
Cheesy mash to serve

1. Season the chicken and wrap it in the prosciutto (around three slices per breast).

2. Add half of the olive oil and half of the garlic to a frying pan, and then add the chicken breasts. Fry on a high heat for three minutes on each side.

3. Take them out of the pan and place them in an ovenproof dish that has been covered with the rest of the olive oil and garlic.

4. Place in a 220°C oven for 20 minutes.

5. Season and serve with green beans and cheesy mash.

# TOP TIP

This recipe is perfect for a date night but involves handling raw meat – if you want the former to go well then you have to be able to do the latter correctly. There's nothing worse than the slow lean in interrupted by food poisoning or worse, a trip to the hospital. Firstly, always store chicken in the fridge, well covered and on the bottom shelf to avoid juices getting on other food items. Secondly anything – anything – that touches the chicken should be immediately washed before coming into contact with anything else. That means your hands, the chopping board, the knife, dishes, etc. Don't wash the chicken itself as bacteria can spread through droplets of water of spray back. Finally, always check that your chicken is cooked and white all the way through before serving and eating.

# ★ HOUSEHOLD HACK ★

In order to stop your showerhead looking like the cliffs of Dover and producing all but a trickle to wash your entire self in, try this next hack. Fill a small plastic bag with vinegar, pull it over the showerhead, fix it in place with an elastic band and leave overnight. The acidity of the vinegar will dissolve the scum that has built up and leave the showerhead looking like new. Remember to run the shower for a little while after you detach the vinegar bag – you don't want to end up smelling like a bag of fish and chips!

# NOTES ON NOTE-TAKING

Note-taking is a practised skill. I started my university life thinking I could transcribe every last word the lecturer said and attempted to dot all the 'i's and cross all the 't's at the same time. However, that didn't work. To start you off in less of a kerfuffle than I was in, here are some tips that should cut down lengthy descriptions and stop your hand from hurting!

★ Use headings to group your notes. Often the lecturer will project a presentation overhead from which you can take inspiration. Think logically and for your future self – what sort of headings will help you to remember the lecture most?

★ When you first start attending lectures, you probably won't know which parts are more important but it's something that can be learnt. For example, as you come to know your lecturer better, you will pick up on key phrases, such as 'another important thing to note' or 'this is particularly vital', that will prompt you to write down the next part. If your lecturer discusses a key person and introduces them with a biography, it's not essential to write down this information if you want a quick break. Instead, jot down their name and add a note to remind yourself to research them after your lecture.

★ Concentrate! Attending lectures is the main reason you are at uni, believe it or not! You can read as many academic books as you like but lectures are often the most effective way of understanding the theories and information you are being taught.

★ Read through your notes after the lecture to ensure that they make sense and that you'll know what they mean when it comes to your revision. Rewrite them, if necessary, while the information is still fresh. Highlight with marker pens the parts that are the most important.

★ Don't write in full sentences but use keywords in succession that will help to remind you of the point your lecturer was making. Don't worry about punctuation or spelling either – even if you're studying English. Use abbreviations to save precious writing time. Here is a list of the most common:

**approx.**  approximately

**b/c**  because

**b/4**  before

**c.**  approximately, roughly, about
(abbreviation for the Latin 'circa')

**cf.**  compared to, in comparison with

**cp.**  compare

**def.**  definition

**diff.**  different, difference

**ea.**  each

**fr.**  from

**gen.**  general

**impt.**  important

**NB**  important, notice this, note well

**nec.**  necessary

**pt.**  point

**re.**  regarding, about

**sim.**  similar

| | |
|---|---|
| **s/t** | something |
| **T.** | theory, theoretical |
| **w/** | with |
| **w/o** | without |
| **v.** | very |
| **viz.** | namely, that is to say |
| **vs.** | against |
| ≠ | does not equal, is not the same as, does not result in |
| ↑ | increase, rise, growth |
| ↓ | decrease, fall, shrinkage |
| ∴ | therefore, thus |
| → | leads on to, produces, causes |
| / | per (e.g. £50/day instead of '50 pounds per day') |

# IT TAKES COURAGE

*to grow up*

## AND BECOME WHO YOU REALLY ARE.

★ *E. E. Cummings* ★

# RECIPE FOR THE TIMES WHEN YOU CAN'T BE BOTHERED TO DO THE WASHING-UP

## NO-STRESS FARMHOUSE FRY-UP
### SERVES THREE

A super-tasty veggie dish for when you're bored of all the instant noodles you've had recently.

## INGREDIENTS

4 tsp olive oil
300 g sliced, parboiled potatoes
250 g mushrooms, washed and sliced
100 g spinach, torn
3 eggs
Paprika, to serve
Hard or Cheddar cheese, grated, to serve
Baguette, torn into pieces, to serve

1. Warm two teaspoons of oil in a pan, add the potatoes and sauté for ten minutes over a medium heat, until browned.

2. Remove the pan from the heat and decant the potatoes into a bowl.

3. Add another two teaspoons of oil to the pan, along with the mushrooms, and place the pan with the lid on over a medium heat for five minutes. Remove the lid, turn up the heat and fry until the mushrooms are browned and there is no liquid.

4. Put the potatoes back in and add the spinach; sauté for three minutes and then break in three eggs. Replace the lid and cook until the eggs have just set.

5. Season with a sprinkle of paprika and top with the baguette and the hard cheese or Cheddar.

# ★ HOUSEHOLD HACK ★

Late for a lecture and can't find anything to shove on? Or perhaps you would have had plenty of time to arrive promptly to your lecture had it not been for the layer of clothes on the floor that is stopping you from getting out the door? Make mornings less stressful with this nifty hack.

When, or maybe more like if, we stack our clothes in piles, the downside is that we have to flip through them in order to find the item we are looking for, which – Sod's Law – is usually at the bottom. Eventually, the pile gets messy and our long-lost best T-shirt sinks to the bottom, never to be seen again until the next big clear-out.

If you arrange your clothes by rolling them and standing them upright in the drawer, you'll be able to see all your items at a glance, and a rainbow of T-shirts will be at your disposal every day.

# TV DRINKING GAME

Great for pre-drinks when you're in your student house, but slightly trickier for those of you in dorms – it might be a squash to all fit in one of your bedrooms, but it's a good way to get to know each other a little better!

DIFFICULTY: ★

This one won't make your eyes go square, but it may make them a bit fuzzy. Great occasions for this game: Eurovision and sporting events, e.g. the World Cup.

Choose a TV show and invent some rules that dictate when players should drink, such as:

★ a given character says their catchphrase

★ you see a scene in a pub

★ you see a certain item of clothing, hair colour, accessory, animal.

If you are struggling, ask your best friend, i.e. the internet, to come up with some for you – there's pretty much a drinking game for everything online!

# Sometimes
## TOO MUCH
## TO DRINK IS
## BARELY ENOUGH.

★ *Mark Twain* ★

# FINDING A PART-TIME JOB

Often your student loan won't get you as far as you want it to and you'll need a part-time job for buying those little extras. Not only is it good for monetary benefits, it will also provide a good example for your CV of how you can juggle your responsibilities, as long as you are managing both well. It may feel a bit daunting to start looking for work in a new, unfamiliar place so here are some tips to get you started.

★ Look on the Student Union web page for vacancies on campus – jobs will usually be within the bar and catering sectors. One benefit of working for your university is that they are more understanding of your workload and should be more flexible with hours than outside companies.

★ Go to your university's careers service – book an appointment with them as soon as you have settled down. They will offer you advice on where to look, as well as give you tips on how to smarten up your CV. Most universities have a jobs portal you can access that advertises local part-time vacancies, some of which are exclusive to students. They can also help you to search for a job that is linked to what you want to do after university.

★ Look for jobs in the run-up to the Christmas period – starting in September, a lot of retailers, restaurants and bars begin advertising temp jobs that usually end on Christmas Eve or after New Year. This is the perfect time to secure a position and if you make a good impression, they could offer you the chance to extend the contract or even make you permanent.

# RECIPE FOR WHEN MONEY IS AN OBJECT AND A VERY PRECIOUS ONE AT THAT

## POTATO AND ONION FRY

### SERVES FOUR

Very cheap and very easy, you probably have most of the ingredients lying around. If you are super-skint, you can spare the extra expense and have it without the bacon.

## INGREDIENTS

1 onion
500 g potatoes
2 eggs, beaten
4 rashers of bacon

1 tbsp plain flour
Salt
Pepper
2 tbsp vegetable oil

1. Peel the onion and potatoes, then coarsely grate them and place in a mixing bowl.

2. Add the beaten eggs, bacon and flour, mix together, and then season.

3. Heat the oil in a frying pan and spoon a series of heaped tablespoons of the mixture into it.

4. Fry the potato cakes on both sides till they turn a golden brown colour. Repeat these steps until all the mixture is used up.

5. Season and serve with baked beans or a salad.

# SAVING WORK LITTLE AND OFTEN

Your brain may be buzzing with ideas and you can't wait to get stuck into the 3,000-word assessment you need to hand in tomorrow, but don't forget to save the document before you start. This needs to be done at some point, so do it before you're pounding away at the keys or your laptop runs out of battery. Then whenever you pause for thought, save save save; it should become an automatic action.

When you start to produce more and more essays, invest in an external hard drive, the cloud or, as a cheaper alternative, send your work as an attachment in an email from and to yourself. There's nothing worse than your computer malfunctioning the moment you're deliriously happy that you have compl— Doh! And you have to start again.

# ★ FANCY DRESS IDEAS ★

## BEACH/HAWAIIAN PARTY

This fancy dress often happens in the depths of winter so don't forget to put a coat on over your scant outfit. If you are stuck for ideas, here is some beach party inspiration.

**1** For girls, a grass skirt is always a good investment (guys, no reason why you wouldn't look good in one either). If you don't fancy wearing a bikini or making your own coconut shell bra, then a brightly coloured top will more than suffice.

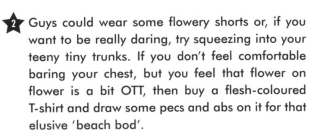 Guys could wear some flowery shorts or, if you want to be really daring, try squeezing into your teeny tiny trunks. If you don't feel comfortable baring your chest, but you feel that flower on flower is a bit OTT, then buy a flesh-coloured T-shirt and draw some pecs and abs on it for that elusive 'beach bod'.

Flip-flops, a straw hat, sunglasses, garlands and a good old inflatable rubber ring or beach ball are all accessories that will add to the effect.

DON'T
EVER
*undervalue*
YOURSELF.

# ★ HOUSEHOLD HACK ★

You've dashed round the supermarket to find the cheapest six-pack on offer and you've returned to find everyone else already pre-drinking. You haven't got time to wait for your beer to gradually cool in the fridge and you can't stand the thought of drinking it at piss-warm temperature. It's a travesty!

But fear not, as here is a quick-fix hack for just such an emergency! Wet a paper towel or kitchen roll, wrap it around your beer can/bottle and place it in the freezer for 15 minutes. When you take it out, the beer will be refreshingly crisp and cold for your delectation.

# HANGOVER CURES DEBUNKED

## *Sleep Tight in Daylight*

## TRUE

There's no particular magic to daytime sleeping itself but sleeping as much as possible the day after drinking will help to cure your hangover. Although we tend to 'crash' when we've had too much to drink, our actual sleep is disrupted by our body's attempt at withdrawing the alcohol. You are permitted to have as many power naps the next day as you like!

# TOP TIP

University can be hard for the kitchen-adverse student, as eating is necessary if you want to live but it will be likely that you don't have the budget for constant takeaway or a generous housemate that's willing to cook for you. If you have either of those things, well done! If not, here are a few top tips to help you cook without the pain. Meals in a mug are excellent quick fixes to get the nourishment you need using a fraction of the time and effort. Another friend to the cooking-phobic are big one pot meals such as chilli. They contain all the goodness you need, require relatively little prep and attention while cooking and can be portioned off and frozen for later. In fact, supersize everything you can and you'll have plenty of leftovers to keep you going. There are lots of great websites that will tell you how long food can be kept in the fridge or freezer.

# RECIPE FOR A TASTY MICROWAVE MEAL IN A MUG

## QUICHE

### SERVES ONE

The quickest quiche you will ever make; it even beats the time it takes to cook a shop-bought one. Great for when you are in a dash.

## INGREDIENTS

- 1 egg, beaten
- ½ tbsp milk
- ¼ of a bagel or similar amount of French bread, torn
- 2 tsp cream cheese

½ slice prosciutto or ham, torn
2 fresh thyme leaves, chopped
Salt
Pepper
Dollop of Dijon mustard (optional)

1.  Mix the egg and milk together with a fork in a mug and season. Tear the bagel or bread into ten-pence-sized pieces and stir into the mixture.

2.  Add the cream cheese to the mix and stir in. Then tear or cut the prosciutto into small pieces and add to the mug.

3.  Sprinkle with the thyme and microwave on a high temperature for about one minute and ten seconds. Season and add mustard on top of your quiche to serve.

# LAPTOP ETIQUETTE

Tap, tap, tap, tap, tap... Tap, tap, tap, tap... Although there are many benefits when using a laptop to record your notes, consider who you are sitting next to and how much noise you make when you type. If you drown out the sound of the lecturer's voice, it's likely your neighbour won't be able to hear much either. If you need a laptop for assistance, consider something that has a quiet keyboard.

Another thing to think about is whether you will be distracted by things on your laptop other than your work. If you know you will be, make sure that you switch off the internet and delete any games before your lecture begins.

# CHALLENGE
## YOURSELF
*every day.* ★ ★ ★

# PERSONALISE YOUR ROOM

Take away the stress of trying to remember what you need to do by making your very own whiteboard – all you need is a photo frame and some pretty wallpaper. Cut the wallpaper to size and place it in the photo frame. Then write and wipe: it's as easy as that! Now all you need is a dry wipe marker and some errands to run!

# ★ HOUSEHOLD HACK ★

Where do all those earring backs, watch screws and contact lenses go when you drop them? I'll tell you where: they're still there; it's just that you're just too blind to see them.

When you drop something small and can't find it, grab your vacuum cleaner and a pair of old tights. Slip the tights over the vacuum nozzle and fix in place with an elastic band. Run the vacuum over the area where you think you dropped your item and, with a bit of luck, it will be sucked onto the tights, where you can pick it off with ease.

# RECIPE FOR WHEN IT'S EXAM TIME AND YOU NEED A LITTLE SPICE IN YOUR LIFE

## VEGETABLE CURRY
### SERVES FOUR

Curry is one dish that most students are familiar with, though not normally when in a state of complete consciousness. There is a wide variety of recipes for curry, but a vegetable curry is both amazingly cheap and suitable for freezing. So why not make a bit extra and save it for when the money runs out mid-term?

## INGREDIENTS

2 tbsp olive oil
1 onion, peeled and chopped
2 cloves of garlic, peeled and finely chopped
1 tbsp madras curry powder
4 potatoes, diced into 2.5 cm cubes
1 leek, sliced
1 tin chopped tomatoes
2 courgettes, sliced
Any spare vegetables
1 dried red chilli
½ pint beef stock
1–2 tbsp water
Salt
Pepper
1 small pot natural yoghurt

1. Heat the oil in a large saucepan and then fry the onion, garlic and curry powder for five minutes or until the onion has softened. Add the other ingredients, except the yoghurt. Season, then bring to the boil, and simmer for 40 minutes or more.

2. Whilst the curry is simmering, taste it to see if it is to the strength required. If it is not hot enough, just add more curry powder.

3. Add the yoghurt five minutes before serving.

4. Serve with rice – if you can afford it, use pilau or basmati rice.

# WHAT THE MIND OF MAN CAN CONCEIVE AND BELIEVE, *it can achieve.*

★ *Napoleon Hill* ★

# REST WELL BEFORE STRESSFUL PERIODS

Your sleeping habits are likely to change when you start university, as too much fun with friends and lots of spare time mean that you can go to bed and get up at ridiculous hours. However, when you are approaching the end of a semester, and your exams and assignments are imminent, you need to try to get into a good routine so that you feel energised and ready to tell those deadlines who's boss. Here are some tips on how to sleep well.

★ Probably the toughest of all the tips in this list, but equally the most important: half an hour before you go to bed, try not to look at any devices that give screen glare, such as phones, tablets and computers. It has been scientifically proven that concentrating on any of these gadgets in the late evening disrupts the body's melatonin production, a key component of your body clock.

★ There is usually some light pollution when it's time to try to get to sleep. Some of it you can't control, such as street lights, but make sure that you sleep in darkness, as you're more likely to wake up in the middle of the night if you have left a lamp on. Even TV stand-by lights can disturb sleep, so always try to turn them off before you get into bed.

★ The temperature of your room can also affect your sleep. It's always better to be on the colder side than baking hot, so don't leave your radiator on when you go to sleep, as you'll wake up in a blistering sweat. Ventilate your room by opening your window during the day and, if you can bear the noisy drunks outside, open your window slightly at night.

★ Don't stress about sleep. Rid your mind of your pent-up worries and, if it helps, buy some essential oils for your bedroom to help you relax. If you find it difficult to stop your thoughts, try visualising a relaxing scene, such as waves lapping or the flow of a waterfall.

# GET YOUR
# S**T TOGETHER

There's a very thin line between messy and MESSY, and most students cross it at some point during their university life. Try to think twice before you reach for that one last Jagerbomb and end up doing one/all of the following things:

★ texting/messaging someone you really shouldn't have – your hot lecturer, for instance

★ throwing up/urinating in something other than a toilet

★ using last night's kebab case as a pillow

★ going to lectures in last night's party outfit

★ throwing an after-party in your tiny dorm without having checked with your roomies

★ waking up with a traffic cone next to your bed.

# PLAN FOR THE FUTURE NOW!

You might think you don't need to start worrying about career options and best ways to secure the job of your dreams until the final year, but this is where many people miss a step. Indeed, in amongst writing your dissertation, studying for exams and doing more essays, you won't have the time to do lots of paid work or volunteering. To help you aim towards a goal, set yourself a yearly plan with targets you need to have completed by the end of each one. Here are some ideas of what you might like to add.

★ Go to a careers fair in **year one** even if you aren't sure what you want to do – it might give you some inspiration. Make sure you engage with employers to get the most out of your attendance. Before you go, create a list of questions you could ask them to help prompt you.

★ Book a careers appointment to discuss job options in **year one**. They will be able to offer information on a whole host of jobs that you might not have even considered or known about before. They can also provide details on job requirements and what preliminary work will help you to boost your chances of getting the position you want.

★ Do at least one week's worth of voluntary work by the end of **year one**. Depending on the company's flexibility, you might have to do a week straight, but more often you will be able to work one day a week. It's always good to stay in contact with the companies you establish relationships with, as they can give you a good reference and might even offer you a job after you graduate.

★ Try to decide by **year two** whether you want to continue studying or go straight into employment after university. Then start researching what this entails – do you need to fill out an application form or are you required to have a certain amount of work experience? Make sure you know all this information well in advance.

★ Book another careers appointment at the beginning of **year two** and try attending regularly so that you can chart your career- or study-seeking progress.

★ Plan to do more voluntary work in **year two**. Try to find new companies to broaden your skill set and opportunities.

★ In your final year, reduce the hours you put into extra-curricular work and focus on your studies, as this is the most important year. However, if you want to do further study, you will need to submit your application form at some point in the year.

# THE ONLY THING
## THAT STANDS BETWEEN
*you and your dream*
## IS THE WILL TO TRY
## AND THE BELIEF THAT IT
*is actually possible.*

★ *Joel Brown* ★

# RECIPE FOR INEXPENSIVE CHRISTMAS GIFTS

## CHOCOLATE TRUFFLES

**MAKES 50**

A perfect gift that's incredibly cheap and very yummy. You can make one batch and give them on separate occasions, plus they are always handy for when you remember someone's birthday at the last minute!

## INGREDIENTS

300 g good-quality dark chocolate,
    70 per cent cocoa solids
300 ml double cream
50 g unsalted butter

1. Break the chocolate into small pieces and tip into a large bowl.

2.  Put the cream and butter into a saucepan, and heat gently until the butter has melted and the cream reaches simmering point. Remove from the heat and pour over the chocolate.

3.  Stir the chocolate and cream together until you have a smooth mixture.

4.  To shape the truffles, dip a melon baller in hot water and scoop up balls of the mixture, or you could use a piping bag to pipe rounds. Lay them on greaseproof paper.

5.  Coat your truffles immediately after shaping; tip toppings (try: crushed, shelled pistachio nuts or lightly toasted desiccated coconut; or even roll a truffle flavoured with orange zest and juice in cocoa powder) into a bowl, gently roll the truffles until evenly coated and then chill on greaseproof paper.

6.  Store in the fridge in an airtight container for three days or freeze for up to a month and defrost in the fridge the night before you plan to give them as presents.

## TOP TIP

To wrap them, place eight or ten truffles in the middle of a piece of cellophane plastic and bring the outer edges together. Secure with an elastic band and tie some ribbon into a bow over it. Keep in the fridge until you're ready to gift them.

*The excellence*
OF A GIFT LIES IN ITS
**APPROPRIATENESS**
RATHER THAN
IN ITS VALUE.

★ *Charles Dudley Warner* ★

# ★ FANCY DRESS IDEAS ★

## RAVE PARTY

The rave party really doesn't go out of style – after all who wouldn't want all the fun of a rave combined with the convenience of being at a club or house party? Rave style is super easy to do and is very easy to adapt depending on your personal style.

★ If you want to go old-school, all you need is a cheap baggy T-shirt, a bucket hat and a whistle hung round your neck. These will all be available cheaply online, or else you can have some fun combing the charity shops for them. A tie-dye or smiley face tee will really evoke the old rave-in-a-field days of the 1990s. Ideally, get a plastic or LED whistle – you're aiming for sick rave rather than sports day.

**2** Buy some UV fluorescent body paints and go to town on your face and arms (and other areas if they're on display!). A stylish swirl of dots about the eyes and brow is a good starting design, but you can do as much or as little as you like.

 **3** Girls, if you're looking for a more modern rave costume, a neon tutu and bikini top combination can look really great. If you're going all in, buy some cheap furry material from the local fabric shop and sew it onto fingerless gloves or leg warmers to complete your look. Guys, it's harder to cheat a good rave look but a neon sleeveless top and some jazzy shades can start you off. If you have the budget, consider stretching to some baggy trousers that you can hang lots of dangly neon and LED accessories off of.

# PREPARE TO GET BATTED!

DIFFICULTY: ★ ★ ★

Set out the pint glasses in two sets of ten, in a triangular 4-3-2-1 formation, at each end of the table and fill them all, at least halfway, with beer. Each player should have an additional drink available for penalties.

Players divide into two teams and position themselves at opposite ends of the table. A player from each team takes their turn to throw their ping-pong ball into any one of the glasses at the end opposite to where they are standing. Every time a team member scores, a member of the opposite team must drink the contents of the cup where the ball has landed. The aim is to eliminate all of your opponents' cups first. If any player misses the cups completely, i.e. the ball lands on the table or on the floor, they must take a drink from their 'spare drink'.

To spice things up a bit, have a few 'killer' cups in each set, containing something like whiskey, vodka or rum.

# ★ HOUSEHOLD HACK ★

Stale snacks are nobody's friend; shoving a handful of crisps or nuts into your mouth only to discover that deliciousness has been swapped for foul chewiness is something no one relishes. Specially made bag clips are available in shops to stop this happening, but why would you buy them when you can have them for free?!

Slide the clips off an old trouser hanger, and use them to seal the bag and keep staleness at bay. You can now open a fresh bag of your favourite snack, safe in the knowledge that you don't have to eat it all in one sitting – unless you really want to.

# THE 'R' WORD

In the run-up to your exams you'll hear the 'R' and 'P' words creeping into conversation in pretty much every sentence. These are: revision and procrastination, the former often leading to the latter. To help you prepare for your exams early, try following these tips.

★ Don't cram all your revision into one sitting the day before. Firstly, nothing will sink in and, secondly, you won't be with it the next day. Plan to start revising well in advance and make a timetable to help you stick to a schedule.

★ Create a comfortable but functional environment to revise in. There's no point revising in a communal area where fun and laughter (and alcohol) will always prevail. Instead, go to the library or sit in your room, but try not to relax in bed while reading or you might fall asleep. Know what's right for you – if you find it easier to concentrate with background noise, play some soft music, whereas if you like silence, it's often beneficial to go to the library.

★ As most revision is done on a device of some sort, it's best to avoid having social media windows in the background. Every five minutes you WILL check what the rest of the world is doing and this WILL take longer to do than the cursory glance you thought you would allow yourself. Sometimes it can even be worth deactivating your accounts during the exam period.

★ The examiner won't see your notes so don't bother making them look neat and pretty – neat for you to understand what they mean is enough. However, use highlighters to colour-code different sections of work that link up with other sections.

★ Don't try to remember long, overly complicated sentences, unless you are memorising quotes from sources – but even then it's best to paraphrase. Write down keywords and link them with arrows to other keywords or whatever works best for you. Flashcards are great; alternatively, buy a pack of Post-its and stick them to your furniture and walls. Make it a ritual that every time, say, you get dressed in the morning or go to bed at night, you read them.

★ Don't make yourself revise so much that you start to look jaded, worn down and, quite frankly, screwed. Give yourself me-time when compiling your timetable and when you do revise, make sure you have a break every hour, especially if you are working at a computer.

# Take a break
## WHEN YOU ARE
## STRESSED
## AND FOCUS ON
## yourself
## FOR A WHILE.

# RECIPE FOR A TASTY MICROWAVE DESSERT IN A MUG

## CHOCOLATE CAKE

### SERVES ONE

Fancy a cake with your coffee or tea but don't want to make a mess? Try this recipe for instant deliciousness and minimal washing-up.

## INGREDIENTS

- 3 tbsp self-raising flour
- 4 tbsp sugar
- 1 egg
- 3 tbsp cocoa powder
- 3 tbsp chocolate spread

3 tbsp milk
3 tbsp vegetable oil
Whipping cream and chocolate sauce, to
serve

1. Put all the ingredients in a large mug and stir with a fork until you obtain an even consistency.

2. Put in the microwave for one-and-a-half to three minutes on the highest setting.

3. Add some whipped cream and a drizzle of chocolate sauce for a truly decadent dessert!

# GET YOUR
≈ S**T TOGETHER ≈

The moment your lecturer asks the class to discuss a certain topic is the time you speak up with confidence and spark a brilliant debate that your lecturer has to end, as class should have finished an hour ago. It is NOT the moment where silence ensues for a good two minutes and your lecturer has to break the deathly quietness with another question that leads to another long, awkward pause. The latter scenario is almost always true but how about bucking the trend and offering your opinion for everyone's sake? This usually leads to other students adding their thoughts to the mix. It might be scary at first, but you'll get used to it quickly enough.

★ **THE** ★
# FUTURE
BELONGS TO THOSE WHO
*believe in the beauty*
**OF THEIR DREAMS.**

★ *Eleanor Roosevelt* ★

If you're interested in finding out more about our books, find us on Facebook at **Summersdale Publishers** and follow us on Twitter at **@Summersdale**.

# www.summersdale.com